CAPPELBAUM'S DANCE

Books by Stanley Cooperman

World War I and the American Novel (1967)
The Day of the Parrot (1968)
The Owl Behind the Door (1968)

STANLEY COOPERMAN

cappelbaum's
dance

UNIVERSITY OF NEBRASKA PRESS · LINCOLN

231154

PS
3553
063
C3

Publishers on the Plains

UNP

Copyright © 1970 by the University of Nebraska Press
All rights reserved
Standard Book Number 8032–0705–0
Library of Congress Catalog Card Number 75–93108
Manufactured in the United States of America

Acknowledgment and appreciation are due the following publications in which the poems listed below first appeared:

Canadian Forum: "Cappelbaum's Valentines"; *Carolina Quarterly:* "Cappelbaum in the Darkroom," "Cappelbaum's Shadow Dance," "Cappelbaum at the Clavichord"; *Chesire:* "Cappelbaum Agonistes"; *College English:* "End of Term in Oregon"; *Concerning Poetry:* "For Marianne Moore"; *Epoch:* "Cappelbaum Among the Cannibals," "Ancestors"; *Extensions:* "For Trudy, Her Fear of Darkness," "Manhattan Transfer"; *The Far Point:* "Two for Freddie"; *First Person:* "Yahrzeit"; *Folio:* "Après"; *The Goliards:* "Cappelbaum in Fun Town"; *Green River Review:* "Ontology"; *Hiram Poetry Review:* "Cappelbaum Hangs Up"; *Hollow Orange:* "Cappelbaum Goes West"; *Jeopardy:* "Cappelbaum Among the Penguins," "Kodachrome for Curmie"; *Jewish Western Bulletin:* "After Watching a Performance of Patelin"; *Kaleidoscope:* "Tasting Jenifer"; *Lillabulero:* "Cappelbaum at the Calliope," "Another Protest Meeting"; *The Nation:* "For Martin Luther King," "Recognition: For Henry Dumas"; *New: U.S. and Canadian Poetry:* "Cappelbaum's Razor-Dance"; *Northwest Review:* "Crusade," "Cappelbaum's Resolution"; *The Outsider:* "Cappelbaum's Halloween"; *Perspective:* "Atrocity! Atrocity!"; *Poet and Critic:* "Cappelbaum and the Carpenter Ants"; *Poetry Bag:* "Cappelbaum's Friday Night"; *Poetry Northwest:* "Hannah's Visit"; *Poetry Venture:* "The Promontory"; *Prairie Schooner:* "Curriculum Vitae"; *Prism International:* "Wallace Stevens is a Fink"; *Quarry:* "Elegy," "Debate With a Writer in Residence," "The Party," "Reverse Plate"; *Queen's Quarterly:* "Chamber Music for Guitar and Hand Grenade"; *Quest:* "Prufrock at the Pentagon," "Cappelbaum's Canticle"; *Quixote:* "Cappelbaum Presents Arms," "Cappelbaum and the Planners"; *South Dakota Review:* "The Engraver"; *Sparrow:* "After the Protest Rally"; *Steppenwolf:* "High Water"; *Stony Brook:* "A Celebration of Headlines"; *Sumac:* "The Dybbuk"; *Talon:* "Cappelbaum and the Serious Woman"; *Tamarack Review:* "Jenifer Waking," "Cappelbaum Murders an Architect," "Cappelbaum's Dance," "Cappelbaum's Confession"; *Trace:* "Cappelbaum Drops Out"; *Unicorn Journal:* "Cappelbaum's Harmonica"; *Works:* "For Alan Watts"

for: Esta
Lil
Jenifer
Galila-Yael
Trudy
Habibi
the Baums
Mike Yates
Brad Cumings
Zorro
Sally
The Cockney Apostle
Mountain Franny
Ziggi
Marya
Ishmael
William Carlos Williams
Sholem Aleichem
The Constipated Jesuit
Hafez
Cathy
Jane
Yandle the Handle
Ann
the Yorkshire Pudding
Ptleman Wasserman
Norman Mailer
The Center Street Jail
Lon Chaney, Jr.
Fred Hampton
Curmie
The Bank of Nova Scotia
Jerry Rubin
Pari
Susi
The Moon Men
Richard III
Nasser
Melina
The Canada Council
The White Knight of Burnaby Mountain
Batman
Radio City
Cricket Lee
Ruth
Mayor Daley
The Tzadek of Minsk
Gollum
Wallace Stevens

and
Samuel Cooperman,
Kester Svendsen: their memory

Contents

Part III

part one

*What do you expect of a man
sailing
by the light of his own wind?*

Cappelbaum's Valentines

i LOVE you.
what does that mean?
I love you.
If I knew what that meant
I would be God
or one of the Directors
of the Esalen Institute.
If I knew what it meant
when I say, when
you say
when they say
I love YOU
in technicolor, with microphones
and fingers, not
a mimeograph machine
in the world
would scare me. . . .

I LOVE YOU
says the man with the brass face.
I LOVE YOUUUUUUUUUUU
says the student screaming on a balcony.
I love you
says the priest, shifting
his pillows.
I LOVE YOU
says the tank commander
in Prague.
I LOVE YOU
says the hand grenade

printed
in the *Berkley Barb*, on green
tissue paper.

They all love me.
They really love me.

What I want
maybe
is to find a place
where nobody
        and nothing
loves me.

Cappelbaum's Dance

Rhythm of words, rhythm of things,
legs under dresses,
bugs
under the sky,
the smell of hyacinths and
old men, both
dying in springtime,
women I don't know, and movies
I missed. . . .

My brain
is a printshop, publishing
inventories,
always a wind

4

blown from my elbows,
and I run,
            I run
up the aisles, plucking
books
and faces
from a million shelves,
without a nickel
to pay the cashier who sits
suspicious
under a red wig,
and tells me to go home.

Every time I breathe
I get hungry,
my eyes
are filled with tapeworms
dancing to a kind of
squeaky drum, daffodils
in my pockets, and
everywhere
store-windows, purple
flowers
just beyond the edge of my tongue:

It's exhausting, this
feeling my hands itch, and
my nose, being
afraid
that cobwebs will grow
between my lips
and yours, thinking
what you would do if suddenly
I climbed under your
shirt,

5

and looked out
from your secret
button-holes, and waved
my fingers
from your throat. . . .

Chamber Music for Guitar and Hand Grenade

Armies never "clash by night";
they do it
in daylight . . . they fill
their eyesockets with blood,
and stomp through the world
with stained glass
hanging from their brains.

Armies are holy things:
properly understood,
a true corpse is a sacramental
candle
burning its own wax
on the high altar of History
and love.

Cappelbaum Among the Cannibals

I
The grand piano in the belly:
mouths
with hairy tongues
hollering for
REAL talk,
girls or critics
with yellow birds
between their cheeks. . . .

Listen, I sniff every petal
with my own nose,
my words
are private as your underwear,
and the sound
of my breath grows
from my skull:

I plant my name
anywhere
          I choose.

Reality? Sincerity? Truth? ??

Let me tell you, my
Reality
changes every time I
eat chicken,
I become something else
with every tit popped

at the sun, and
sometimes
there are grapes I peel
with the teeth
of my brain.

Don't tell me what SINCERITY
is, I carry it around
in my pants, under my collar:
whatever I say is made of paint
and kisses,
greasy dreams and REASONS
that grow like crabgrass on a pile
of cut
        poems.

II
Part of me is the splinter
under my toenails:
when I open my
voice, rabbits
eat pomegranates on a silk bed,
unicorns
raise their legs,
dying
under a shower of
apricots. . . .

what do you expect of a man
sailing
by the light of his own wind?

Let me tell you about
TRUTH:
it dances on the edge
of becoming, it
foams
on an ocean
of everybody's water turning
to air. . . .

Truth swims under the shadow
of stones,
like our faces
when we float toward each other
inside our separate balloons;

Truth is nothing, everything
that won't stand still for you,
for me, or the man
with cotton proclamations
wrapped
around his balls. . . .

WHY
should I swear who I am
when the whole thing
is not to decide

on this side of the grave?

Jenifer Waking

To drift is no
meaning: neither tree
nor root, and shapes of earth
held
in the circle
of your eye, are less
than light: an electric bulb
plugged
into stone.

Today
when you half-slept
in your skin,
putting on your robe,
drifting into the green light
of morning,
there was a rose
framed
in the small window
under your breast.

To drift
is no meaning: only
when I looked at you,
light
flowed green
between us: the glass
melted, the stone
dissolved
into white silk.

For Martin Luther King

The blood will continue:
and words
falling
like dead animals
in the green pastures
of his Lord;
all around his secret
fear, the Book
he carried in his brain,
other men
         dreamed
of corpses
dancing in a strobe-light
of History and skin.

He was not
         romantic
enough: too slow
for running. Someone
could not
forgive him that.
He never
changed his name, or swore
return
to any other land. . . .
reason enough
for some Hero of metal
to rip him down like a flag
unmasted

when it was rising
at last
to the sun he praised.

High Water

It begins with a pause:
like breath
puffed across a candle,
a rhythm of objects
unmoving
in a square of empty space, the brain
oiled ready to receive mermaids
or salt nails. . . .

It begins
with oceans pouring from the dark
side
of your eye, a tide
rising between the hooked fingers
of logs, their shapes
eaten
by hysterical birds. . . .

Sometimes
it begins with color: red
spray
breaking from a pier,
an eruption of twisted
leaves, seaweed

12

hanging
from an open cave. . . .

Or wind:
in the valley between words,
in the rockfall yellow
rattle and
bang
of a smile, when suddenly all
you want to do is grab hold,
like a man dissolving

dissolving
into green snow, or flowers
heavier
than hailstones.

For Marianne Moore

This is permissible: to use
quotation
            marks
like small flowers, and
to throw them
over the wind,
            plucked:
a rain of purple leaves
from the mouths
of a thousand libraries,
lions

in white boots
              dancing
behind the garage. . . .

Old women
who rollerskate through the world
on wheels of paper
do this: nibbling
bridges, animals, dead poets
and gardens,
sometimes a wild flea
turning
         to acid
in a pot of Japanese
tea.

Lady, your lips
are thin
as lace, and your songs
fall quietly
into my brain, like
plums
        of ice.

The Dybbuk

There is something
in me, pressed
from the meat of my lungs,
breath

pushing under my skin,
opening and closing:
a fist
toughened by salt blood,
and vessels beaten
into the shape of disaster
        or love.

Sleeping, talking, reaching
out with the red horn
of my thighs,
blowing swollen air
onto this paper, filling
the space
between our names,
I feel knuckles: they strike
fire
on the bone
behind my tongue,
and I celebrate, fear
the metronome of my own wind,
a burning glass driven
into my skull. . . .

and yours:
because when I spread
red
syllables into space,
when I take you by the roots
of your eyes, crying
TRUTH, like a drunken priest
trying
to baptize the moon,

I hold the juice of dreams
in the palm of my brain,
the jokes
you will never see:
how everything we believe
must kill us with
health, like

that blind muscle
squeezing
under your ribs
between kisses, dinners, and
    parades.

Wallace Stevens is a Fink

"Poetry is the supreme fiction, Madame."
                              —W. Stevens

Supremacy? look: I hold on
to my eyeglasses
with both hands, like
a man dying
on roller-skates,
or a lover
swallowing his own seed,
nauseated by the
cannibal
inside his mouth.

I once knew a man
taller
than the top
of his head; he spent
the secret coins
of all his days on slot-
machines,
waiting for the jackpot, a poem
to leap yellow and
singing
out of his face. . . .

he was killed
tripping
on a hockey stick,
and when they carried him
out of the world,
ice-cubes
fell from his pockets
like used
          books.

Ancestors

"My father was a long-nose,"
          said the man who sold ice-cream.
"My father was an oxygen tank."
          "My father was a broken violin."

In the days of poetry-by-the-sea
when cellar clubs blossomed red and green
along Ocean Parkway,

in the days of truant sunlight and bifocal deans
who found unused but hopeful prophylactics
in bar-mitzvah wallets,
my old man offered me a ten-pound hammer,
love and curses in four slavic languages,
and told me to show Black Jimmy
who (sometimes) fought main events,
that a gahlitz could beat the disadvantage
of having dreams.

I took the hammer, I told my fingers to be hard,
I cut through the soft white leather
and the mirror of his eyes;
but the shoes were
for babies who could not walk
and I hated the blonde women of Wisconsin
who would take them to some confirmation,
love among the wheatfields,
while Label and Mr. Shavelson crouched over their
                                                    machines

like fat fates, and the blue-bald myopic eyes,
the delicate soft fingers,
plucked white skin to survive in the promised land
of Brooklyn.

One foot withered in the shank
in the time of his button-hole days, my father said
remembering white-wolf rolling country
and the bold horsemen
planting their hooves on the quake of his brother
as the black-bellied stove threatened
to set fire to Mr. Murphy,
who came with a gust of great Goddamns
and a walking stick,
who challenged Black Jimmy to a Ukraine wrestle,

who was loved for his 80 years
of joyous and syphilitic life.

And we corrupted the tight, futile little shoes
onto wooden lasts
becoming splinters against each other,
demanding something else,
an end to kosher meat for example,
until I struck him from the list of my love
because I met T.S. Eliot
looking for stained glass on the Brighton Express,
and those were samovars that were his lips.

Surely there must be ancestors
and they are not to be found in San Francisco;
I remember the eyes of a dying man and nothing
                                behind them,
I cannot remember the name or nature of his brittle flesh,
only a set of German philosophers
shaking like dry leaves,
turning to beards and dust beneath my lids
while somebody's mother and three white shoemakers
howled in the front room,
and panicked ribs drew blood from my hands.

My father, listen:

    I would be proud to stand beneath the canopy
    of your twisted body and the voice of your eyes;
    I would weep for the least knuckle of your anger.

The Party

Carrying a lollypop
and two
        bananas, she
drifts
into the room with a yellow
wig   oozing
from her skull:
her mouth stretches
like torn
        plastic, something
feathered, or a ball
bouncing
on the tip of her voice.

She walks
like a little girl
with cotton-
candy
between her legs, everything
sticky and
good: butterflies
drown
in the sweat
of her charms, and moths
drop from her thighs.

Her costume is
a nightgown
of pink rubber, it
glistens
like spilled beer, and

her teeth move
                    slowly
through the air,
leaving a taste of sucked
grapes, their skin
smoother
than a smile.

End of Term in Oregon

(for Kester Svendsen, my Father-in-Law)

We are all terminal cases:
the breath
                    dancing
in our mouths
burns
what is uses: like
those trees
twisted
with living
against the wind, eaten
by sunlight
and salt.

I can tell you
                    nothing
except
that we stand
on the same coast,
drinking

the same fire :
  liquid
          ripped
from the skin
of a dying star.

Yet
washed with that death,
here
        on my window,
are green leaves
smaller
and more helpless
than a kiss :
look
at the way
they swallow galaxies. . . .

Know this : it was
from you, the distance
of a touch
light-years
away from now, that
Jenifer
          happened :
the beginning
of my growing
into love.

Cappelbaum's Parable

I once knew a traveler
who waited, loaded
with empty suitcases,
for a Great
Thing:
but the machine
was blind, switched
on
a dead track.

Filled
with steam and indignation,
the loca-
motive
pumped
T
R
U
T
H
from all its boilers, and
fell into a river. . . .

The man stood there
seriously
in a closed station, until
his fingers
stretched
into iron railings,
and his eyes flattened
in his head, like
green
        flags.

23

For Alan Watts

Flushed to the end, guru:
your mouth opens like a blinker
and your eyes are broken
circuits, like
when you jet in from LA
goosing buddhas and drinking
lotos-juice with the girls:
electric lamb-chops
fall out of the sky, Saints
cross their testicles
with moonlight
and magic chicken-soup. . . .

I want to know
what
you taste
at night, when your private moon
is wrapped in cellophane,
and your tongue grows thick
behind your teeth, and
God
blows into your room
like a torn branch.

Cappelbaum Murders an Architect

"I want to borrow some
of your insanity,"
he said, lifting
the top of his skull
like a geodesic dome, and
staring
in a vulgar way
at the owl
pinned to my left buttonhole.

He told me about his dream
of dead elephants,
dogs
eating frozen turds
in an arctic jungle,
where bananas
hang from the nostrils
of permafrost cannibals.

What could I do?
I mean, there
he was, like a rosebush
brittle
at both ends, an icicle
hammered into my crotch,
or a steel
          finger
pointing at my head.

DON'T BREAK MY EYEBALLS
I shouted,
squirting him
with flower juice:
and when he died,
I wrapped him in cellophane,
stamped him
with flat stones, and
mailed him
all the way to next year.

Prufrock at the Pentagon

(October 21, 1967)

And there was Robert Lowell
wearing the bottoms of his trousers
horn-rimmed, with a copy
of *The New York Review*
rolled between his good intentions. . . .

Draping his ancestors over marmorial
memorials, he agreed quietly
to join the Good Guys,
but found a certain difficulty
in Virtue, which sweated
on the trees, and the grass, and Norman Mailer,
and the square pool, and Sister X,

when her voice
jackbooted the crowd:
ten thousand mouths
filled with the broken wind of Armageddon.

Clutching a microphone, looking embarrassed
at the food hustlers, remembering
Denise, who warned poets against
talking
when truth demands BODIES, feeling his hair
so thin that each New England follicle
accused his skull,

did he cherish
a modest crucifixion,
or roll his eyeballs
down the bowling alley of History?

What was it like, Robert Lowell,
to be an immigrant at last,
in that country where the only heroes
are wrapped in cellophane, and sold
for two bits and a busted guitar?

Cappelbaum's Canticle

there is a party tonight.
my wife is angry because I read poems
without money,
and there is a party tonight.

the snow is covering the mountains,
and there is a party tonight.
the snow covers the mountains
without money,
the samovar must be polished,
rugs cleaned, the wine
must be spiced
because there is a party tonight,
and the snow
falls on the mountains, I
fall on the mountains
like pieces of torn money,
past sea gulls and whales, past children
who want to talk about poems
and universities
without money, they forget
that there is a party tonight,
they exploit me,
they sell my bones for ikons
in the Community Center,
where ladies
come to me holding out their deaths
and wrinkles,
asking me to explain
without money, why the snow
falls on them
when there is a party tonight,
when there are
always
parties tonight, and the snow

    in the mountains
    fills the empty pockets of my skin
    with wads of wet poems
    and no money.

Surrealism : A Lecture On

Kangaroos and ice-cream cones:
everything
is magic, like
    sawdust
swimming
in the green sea,
or dolphins
leaping down Granville Street
tickled with smog.

Where you are is the actual
laughter
of be : your hand
wiggling
at the tip
of your bones, holding
a newspaper, or
me.

Debate with a Writer in Residence

My residence
is in my skull:

a mouth filled with white
thorns, newspapers,
honey
pasted to the dreams of a woman,
when she spreads
red hair
on the last pillowcase
of God.

My residence
is in my skull:

a boy
running braindeep in plums,
each step
sucking him down,
        sucking him down
to a room
filled with laughter,
an inch of wax
held
in both hands.

My residence
is in my skull:

a thief
nailed to a shell of bone
softer
than his shadow:
a lover
feeling a small contraction
behind his retina,

when he squirts
both
eyeballs
at the moon.

Cappelbaum and the
Carpenter Ants

Who stole the pearls
from the oysters
under my pillow?
Even in dreams, I hear
shells
      cracking
louder than kisses,
a kind of petrified dandruff
scratching
the back of my mind.

Staring at the roof
I see black
ants
big as my toe
marching out of the light bulb,
chomping on shadows
with frankenstein teeth;
they run up my pajamas
at 40 miles a minute, looking
for unoccupied skin.

Thieves! Goniffs!
pearl-robbers!
Listen: give me sea-monsters, give me
the moon
nailed to my forehead,
          give me
green snails, giraffes
dancing
on broken feet:
anything but these crazy animals
who don't know a Solid
Scholar
when they see one. . . .

Atrocity! Atrocity!

Driving through New Mexico
in a flower-wagon,
I was
          scalped
by a drunken policeman;
Hoohah, Yoiks, Yeah-Yeah
he shouted,
driving me out of Taos
with a brace of blue dogs
on a leather leash; and
when their teeth
snapped
at my elbows, I thought of calling
on Leroi Jones, all

his 300 years:
but I dusted Auschwitz
from my collar
and apologized
for the outrage of
New Jersey. . . .

Being a coward and a Jew
guilty
of existence,
all I could do was
wish for a black skin
or a brown or even a little bit
chocolate, so I could
suffer
          legitimately;
somehow it seemed
like Russia
again,
when the poor peasants
hated the Czar, and dreamed
of burning his palace down,
but broke
the fiddle of my Uncle Louie instead,
because
it was so much closer,
and maybe
          out of tune
anyway. . . .

Believe me, it's been a lousy
3,000 years: running
all the way
either toward Revolutions
or away from them.

33

Recognition : For Henry Dumas

"On Thursday, May 23, one of our editors was shot to death on a New York City subway platform. His name was Henry Dumas [a black poet]. The man who shot him was a Transit Authority policeman."
Editorial, Hiram Poetry Review

In the beginning
there was fear: my father
spoke to me
of a crucifix
driven
into an infant's skull, while
the priest
drooled Jesus, and women
twined flowers
in his beard.

In the beginning
there was fear: white wolves
whose jaws
were filled with icons,
red faces
open like a furnace,
and each Gentile handshake
was a handful
of burning coal.

In the beginning
there was fear: I ran
through streets
of iron windows, flesh
so alien

I could not imagine
that it lived on human bones:
a time of taverns
and graveyards.

I remember that beginning, I
remember, and now
only
        sometimes
do I fear the beginning
just begun.

part two

Everywhere I go
there are crazy animals
spitting
iron peanuts
at the stars

Cappelbaum and the Serious Woman

No, I won't march
from Viet Nam
into your bed: balling
has a different sort
of politics,
and when I smell mimeo-
graph ink
in the corners of your mouth,
I feel ice cubes
drop
down the front of
my pants. . . .

Listen: necrophelia is
bad enough
when it's personal,
but this long-distance
commitment
growing over the sweet edge
of your honeypot means
dryness, like
my tongue suddenly
too small
for your indig-
nation. . . .

No
I won't march:
find someone else,
a poet
with a blue cape and HISTORY
hanging from
his crotch, who gets
an erection
every time he passes a fire. . . .

Me, I won't settle
for stones, and when
oranges
and yellow birds
fall out of the sky, I sing
wedding music
here,
        now:
the sound of mountains
smaller
than my pulse.

Reverse Plate

There is a great poison
on the wind
and the trees know it,
the trees
in their green
burning
        know
what poison means,

how
invisible
beyond the knowledge of
bombs
       or poets,
a great poison
gathers
in the shadow
of dahlias,
under the eaves of books
where no shelter
is, a thin
scream
of mimeograph machines,
indignations
clotted
with perpetual
     August
in the brain.

There is a great poison
on the wind
and the trees know it,
their roots
         fall
from the air
like marching leaves,
an inversion
clenched
into a grip
of black
and irresistible
fire.

Cappelbaum in the Darkroom

Why
should the shape of a breast
be printed?
under your fingers
the bright napalm of earth,
the soft mouths
of women or trees,
become arrangements of acid:
a room
filled with glass.

No:
I will open my veins
to every thorn,
in gardens
where flowers and lovers
are rotten with scent. . . .
I will hang from my feet
and wave my eyes
at the sun.

A bird
worn in the buttonhole,
an owl dancing
wing-deep in
mud,
are greener than all the neon
fires of your mind:
and the smallest
aphid
eats roses
all the way to December.

The Engraver

To set down small
things: broken
crystal, or a brown dog
sleeping
on a couch. . . .

the exact shape
of the skin
around your mouth,
your after-dinner smile
melted
into coffee and steam. . . .

a bookcase, the sound
of breath
around the corner
of a glance, or

the way a chair stands
firm,
knee-deep in space. . . .

This
is more difficult than
mountains, which
need
        nothing.

Curriculum Vitae

The green leaf moves
and the poet dies,
his mouth a darkness
filled with names,
unwritten love
that we must prize
through his imagination,
not our own; blame
the wind for this,
or the dumb earth
that eats poets
words and all; curse
the Bibliographer, his mind
that buries poets
with their kind.

The Prophet

With aromatic tongues
I have come to give testimony:
the ape
in the garden
buried
with the holy shawl
of my father,
who fell out of the world,
in the Canal Street subway,

complaining
that unkosher wolves
were eating his brain.

Testimony, I have come to give
    testimony:
before every altar
I will set a yellow bird
and a painted rooster,
until eggs like
rainbows
        leap
from the Rabbi's beard
when he raises his scroll. . . .

a bloodstone
for each of his fingers,
sabbath silver
woven
into prayers for the dead.

Cappelbaum Hangs Up

My pockets are too small.
My feet make lumps in them
every time I stomp along Second Avenue
among French restaurants and discreet
clubs. Sometimes
I feel my nose grow wet under my shirt.

It depends on the way you walk.
That's what they say.
If you walk naturally,
with your beard pointing at the ground,
you won't see children pounded into the sky
like chow-mein on a tablecloth.

The good things will be there:
old furniture, and poodles, and St. Patrick's
squatting on Fifth Avenue
with gold paint
sprayed over the Virgin's tits. . . .

But my clothes are tight.
My collar turns into iron spikes
that catch me behind the knees,
and my legs swing East
and West
whenever I catch a crosstown bus.

Listen: who wants to greet his neighbors
through holes in their socks,
or say HELLO
to that jovial cop
with teeth snapping from his zipper?

It's not easy, it's not easy,
knowing that my brain is getting bald,
that my eyebrows
are freezing to the pavement,
that my lips are stuck
to all the little red wagons of Christmas.

After the Protest Rally

And always the scream:
the corpse dancing with books
hanging
like iron bells
from the joints of his bones,
a smell
of rotted machines
turning to grass,
                        turning to grass
or proclamations
thin
as the flower
growing out of his eye.

When I walk though the street
there are old women
crucified
on telephone wires,
a sound of humming in the air
like mumbles of thick
laughter: and priests
with hooks
curved to the ends of their arms. . . .
they hang
from their own blackness.

Even the snapdragons
bite one another,
fighting for room, fighting
for a deeper swallow
of light and air:

47

their colors
hammer the summer sun
with a fire of painted
teeth.

A Celebration of Headlines

This
above all things
delights me: the holy
transubstantiation, boiling
in the dark cup, the greasy
miracle
of the mind. What
we are, surprises me less
than that cat
asleep
in a thick chair, who
is always
            cat, always
without malice,
always
boring as hell, except
for a certain temperature
of blood or purr.

We
on the other hand
explode in the corners
of our flesh

like possible firecrackers
fused with death.
Put two of us in a room, and
BANG
        we happen,
a rotten arithmetic
of stars and bananas,
trees
made into poems,
interplanetary gas
erupting
as flowers, or woolen hats,
or Virtue,
        or bombs. . . .

all the suspense
of being
        printed
in a limited
edition
of breath.

Crusade

Oozing a red
moon from his mouth,
the guardian of proper
        motivations
demands FREEDOM
and walks redeemed
among corpses

49

of the unworthy. . . .
slogans print themselves
in his eyeballs, mimeo-
graph DENUNCIATIONS
of imaginary popes
and everywhere
big bellies, fat
women,
PEDOGOGIC PRINCIPLES
mocking the holy orifice
of history.

    Don't joke
with this man
boy,
don't tweak his
ponderables, or sing
unmeaning
lyrics before breakfast;
distribute
        something,
badge yourself seriously
and refrain from yessing
grapes or unwithered
plums;
tear out your teeth
lest they offend
with laughter,

and from the empty cave of your lips
be content to suck
    TRUTH, like
a stone lollypop was
stuck
in your face.

50

On Hearing a Lady Poet's Recipe for a Lover

Because he would lurch through a woman's mind
trailing his own intestines
from his mouth, his eyes,
the man with the blue statue
stood on street corners
blowing fig leaves in every direction.

With a blue statue in one hand
and the thigh of a wild bird in the other,
his fingers were thin songs,
and his bones
vibrated
like the strings of a pawnshop guitar.

But nobody loves a beggar,
not even those who throw coins at him,
and if a man stand in a public place
with a blue statue
jigging
on a wire,
let him dance for nickels and dimes.

    Lady, I agree:
    why give your flesh to an empty man,
    when the full
    are firm and lovely in your arms?

Cappelbaum Among the Penguins

Zoo-brother, I ask you:
which lion
do you want me to grab
by the skin, what
ape
can turn bananas into swans
through the magic
of his gut?

Everywhere I go
there are crazy animals
spitting
iron peanuts
at the stars: they show me
documents,
identity-cards, and ask
me to produce my own.

What should I give them?
a testicle
soaked in gasoline?
the band-aid I wear
over the scraped
edge
of my brain? a mortgage
to guarantee clear title
on my cage?

All I have is a trick
made of frozen jello: I keep it
moving
by an act of breath, and
pump empty space
from one side of my chest
to the other.

Why
should I tie black balloons
to my feathers?

Cappelbaum Goes West

Like a horse, a blue
horse
with a mouthful of flowers
is the sound of time
in my head. . . .
but something moves
under my skin, tumbles
on mountains,
the secret trails
chopped
into my heart.

Between my left hand
and my right hand
is a stable: its walls
are hung with saddles
nobody
will ever use,
and there are rats
who make crooked bets
in the unclean
straw.

Listen:
what do leaves taste like?
the sun?
pigeons dancing
on corners of the moon?
Why am I obsessed with
horses,
their stupid hooves,
and the way
they turn flowers into dung?

Manhattan Transfer

Music
      sewn
out of brass and dead trees:
switchblades
hidden
behind the fat smell
of a lilac.

It's a question
of symbols, if you
look for them:
snow
between the paws
of a young dog,
when it limps
over chemicals and theaters,
a pavement
hardened with money. . . .

or the girl
hustling Fourteenth Street
with each breast
candy-
        flavored, brown
stones
tied to her nipples:
they swing
            they
stretch splat against the wall
of KLEIN'S, and

whisper
        juicyfruit
in a nickel bag of love.

Another Protest Meeting

Here are my fingers:
ten columns of smoke
blown across your face,
and a mouth
filled with broken bones.
What war are we fighting?
I look at you, and see
a crazy frontier:
barbed wire
thicker than jungles.

Your words float toward me
like swollen glands: they
bust
into something yellow
when I touch them,
and suddenly
everything I know about love
becomes a foetus
soaked
in burning gasoline.

Cappelbaum in Fun Town

The diplomat flowing past the curb
bobbed like an orange
and spat seeds
across First Avenue: his secretaries
rolled up their garters
and nailed themselves to the wind
blowing
from an air conditioner
of the Beaux Arts Hotel.

It was a hot day
for February:
poodles with old men in their jaws
tied ribbons for the canopy
of Gatsby's saloon, and a missionary
demanded full
membership
in the United Nations as a
      CONDITION
of Moral Unarmament.

Why not? I mean, no man
is a traffic island,
and the funny exhaust pumping from his brain
made carbon particles that I still
breathe
every time I open a newspaper:
even my lungs wrinkle
headlines
under my shirt.

So I stopped a policeman,
and offered
to donate my tapeworm collection
to the CIA; but he
threatened me with a fistful of lottery tickets,
and chewed me around the corner
with each of his buttons
clenched
into broken teeth.

Being 39 years of age, and
in lousy health, I knew when I wasn't wanted;
I saddled my dog
and rode toward the crabgrass
of Sutton Place, but
a man screamed at me
for stomping his favorite fez,
and two airline stewardesses,
with smiles
hanging from their seatbelts,
accused me of following them
into the ladies' room of St. Patrick's.

That's why I'm hiding here, under
the city desk
of the *New York Times :* it's a matter of
not
getting into trouble
                    with anyone.

Cappelbaum's Turntable

It is easy to talk
believe me,
    easy
to pluck rainbows from the eye-
brows
of strange women,
find magic
    in wild fleas,
or wait for Roman coins
to hatch
under your mattress.

What really matters is the
fact
that you eat air,
a space
vibrating between your lips
for no reason, like
apricots
tossed at the moon,

and after you push
just so many
shapes
      around, the problem
is to look at your shoes and find
your own feet,
because
they get stiff after a while,
like twigs
that break at the first
sign of snow:

face it. Toes are always
ugly, especially
when you forget them,
and spend all your
          time
dancing
    on your mouth.

Still Life : A Demonstration

A room, a table, a blue bowl
in whose second skin
bulks a container
contained
by silver and light,
an alloy of pressed function :
granules of tin,
aluminum glued
to something like metallic
glass. . . .

the pulp it cups
is the masticated garbage
of machines, but well-
watered, it   resembles
earth.

In that substance
propped,
are ferns stirred by fingers
of sudden color,
yellow fists : a kind of sun-
flower, but without
the roasted seeds
that old men
crack between their teeth.

Then
        a trinity
of carnations tipped with
holy blood,
waiting
for a ceremony
of hooded bees to descend
through the window,
where forests of boys
dream of firecrackers and
cats. . . .

meaning nothing less,
and for no
reason,
than the shape of what
and where is
not
        you.

Cappelbaum's Friday Night

Somewhere
a rabbi is singing tonight:
his brain is brown
with joy, Truth
stains his fingers,
and a bride
sets a white cloth
for the Sabbath
ceremony
of her skin. . . .

There is a mist in this room.
Blood.
Frogs.
Locusts.
There is a mist in this room.

Stained
glass? illuminations
at midnight? Here:
I offer you unblessed bread
to chew
with all the gums
of your soul, and Love
like a plucked chicken
dancing
on its own feathers.

Cappelbaum and the Planners

I came across the President
of the Ladies
                    Auxiliary
rubbing herself
with the urine of pregnant
mares. . . .
what sort of thing
is
   that, for a Jewish mother
to squeeze?

I mean, interfaith festivals
aside, there are
lions growling
on the scrolls of the Law,
pulling their beards
with uncut
claws, and if such
methods
are allowed between the sheets
of sanctified dreams,
where will our
FUTURE be?

Anyway, what sort of
goniff
gets those mares pregnant?
Where does he live?
Something tells me that the
          Rabbi
is involved with the whole business:
I saw him last Saturday night

slouching
past the Country Club, hanging
around
      the stables
with a strange Social Worker
on each arm. . . .

On Watching a Performance of *Patelin* by the San Francisco Mime Troupe

In a pool of melted flesh I see them,
shapes of old beards and holy fire;
their arms hang from a landscape
of broken trees, and from their arms
a ram's horn screams into the face
of God.

Here the audience has firmer bodies:
skin stretches neatly on their bones,
flesh dances with Revolution,
love, *Judendreck*, and laughter. . . .
the symbolic JEW, boiled in the grease
of his own blood.

    In a pool of melted flesh I see them,
    shapes of children and holy fire;
    their arms hang from a landscape
    of broken trees, and from their arms

a hook-nosed angel with burning wings
spits at the face of this History,

our God.

Cappelbaum at the Calliope

Clown and tiger
now
    we rehearse
the corners of an empty stage;
like a wheel
    or flash of coins
in our heads,

metal
on blue wood,
we toss ourselves at the sun
driving machines
                    and stars
for un-
written parts, laughter
breaking from the

            galleries, there: gold

falling with applause
and women, jade
mice
running up and down their
            throats. . . .

Top banana, each of us,
twirling
wet moustaches,
Desdemona climbing
through Hamlet's window,
unwed mothers
hiding in Charlie Chaplin's pants, and

we wait
to be born
again, between the acts,
rolling down mountains
we have never
                climbed,
horses
with yellow paint on their hooves:

always
the soliloquy,   here

now   at the edge of our eyes

        while the swift hiss of God
        hurts us, like

        silence. . . .

part three

Why are those bits of burning hair
blowing
from your mouth?

Cappelbaum Presents Arms

When I crouch
inside my head, and look
at the world
through eyeballs
swollen
with yesterday's wind,
all I can see
is a forest of boiled
glands:
I WANT, like
spiders
trying to eat stones.

I listen to you, I
listen, I
try
not to choke on the smoke
pumping
out of your brain: I break
my fingers, so I can walk
up to you, and say. . . .
look: I have no
fists,
I can't fight anybody
with the stumps
of my hands.

Yahrzeit

Since there is no color
in your memory,
and stems
have whitened
beneath the borders
of your eyes,
water
grown heavy
with the death of clouds,

I offer you this
    seed
of other harvests,
crops of husband-
ry and gardens,
trees
dark with fruit;

walk in the shade of peaches
round
as the sky,
the sun on your mouth,
and a voice
filled with names carved
on a carnival tent;

remember
the river
of blue snow
piercing your arms,
ice
and honey

stretched between two hills
in a sleep
soft as yellow
hair. . . .

That hand on your chest
has its landscape
too, the juggler of
white knuckles,
    flowers
hard
    as teeth.

Cappelbaum Agonistes

Yes, I send telegrams to myself
now and then,
but only when the moon
is out: it's
a ritual,
my own little
ritual,
because the whole bit
stimulates me, all
those crazy rocks
with bad skin
and gas
whirling around the gut
of God
(the old man

who kills chickens
on Brighton Beach Avenue
and never feels
guilty)

Me, I like to think
about the moon
swinging
up
          down
there, round
or maybe like sour cream
in the sky,
and every time I
think
of the moon
I get horny, which
believe me
is a great relief
considering how many girls
nowadays have
petitions
(that they write THEM
SELVES)
between their kisses. . . .

Give me the moon every
time, and a good
finger
that I can play
like a violin.

Elegy

It is quiet now,
the stars
and my pulse,
                    quiet
as wet grass is
quiet,
          filled
with the frozen worms
of November.

And this day
I have struck down everything:
the candle in my bones,
the green leaf
growing
in my brain,
                    a man
whose work I broke, seeing
in his eyes
the stamp of my own
death. . . .

And this day also
I have done
strategy, planned action
and response, sold
whatever there was to be sold,
borrowed
               kisses
from a dying
animal:

```
                only
     there is this voice
     screaming from
     somewhere:
     a mouth filled
     with iron flowers,
     an echo
     of something
                hard.
```

Ontology

```
The lullaby of
green
is what
I am after:
through the
laughter
of earth and eye-
balls, something
rounder
than historical lovers
when they rush
screaming
over the concrete
pastures
of the sky, because
our kisses
are more than
ropes
```

74

tying our brains
together, more
than any cloud
of gnats
with sticky halos
on their wings. . . .

my fingers
see
the shapes
          singing
in the throat
of unplucked weeds.

Hannah's Visit

Like Sabbath flowers
sewn
to the jaw of an old man, for
decoration, for love. . . .
or a nightingale
plucked
to its poor wrinkled skin,
she enters
the deepest room
of your skull
with all her fingernails broken
into colored paint, and
sits
holding
the points of her knees.

75

Eggs
fry in the corners of her smile,
their yolks screaming
conceptions
at midnight, when thighs
open, and owls
hunt
        mice
in her pubic hair;
her voice circles
once
or twice, and lands
on the knobs of its claws
in the middle of
little boys
rubbing themselves all over the rug.

Is she pregnant?
will her father ride
black
horses
on her best friend's bed?
why have her teeth
turned into glass,
and who polished her brain
until it gleams
in a knot
of crooked mirrors?

Kodachrome for Curmie

Color, color, color:
what I want is a rainbow
of tangerines and whales,
God
with a barber-pole
in each fist,
dancing
with yellow boots
through the parking lot
of his own beard. . . .

Give me a can of paint
and a good mule
and I'll turn your pores
into polka-dots and
daffodils,
stones
that swim in the green sea,
salmon leaping
out of blacktop roads. . . .

Kingfishers and toads
slap all their skins together
for a lightshow
fire
hotter than the stars.

Après

In my garden
snow has turned to ice on the flowers.
On the small, white flowers
the snow
is heavier than history or love.
Spring comes down from the mountains
with a smell of evergreens,
the salmon
are stirring in the muddy sea,
but the snow turns to ice
on the flowers in my garden,
and the children
home from school, spurting
out of school
with their voices and glands,
rattle on the fence
at the edge
of my garden, where white
    flowers
are crushed by ice.

Cappelbaum in the Colony:
Waiting for Icarus

In the mountains
girls with tight pants
dream

of exploding stars, eeeeeeeeeeee
Ching,
the sacred mushroom
until September, when
back
to campus
go anthropology instructors,
chicks thinking
lighshows, Danny
        Boy
and the truth
about Paris.

Me, I stand there
stumped
on a dead tree, waiting
for bugs
to jump out of my eyelids, or
that Holy Shlemiel
from Brooklyn, with a beard
like a used *talis:* he's
OMing himself
around the fire
stroking
both his tambourines. . . .

Next morning comes
onion stew
THE BREAKFAST OF CHAMPIONS
cracking like glue
in unwiped pots;
a slum goddess
from Scarsdale swings
yellow hair,
praying to petrified bones

mounted
on the pole of her tent
(and the Lone
     Ranger
rides her blue horizon
over the Apache mud
of her mysteries)

—Boulder, Colorado: 1967

For Trudy, Her Fear of Darkness

Even sunlight
breaks
into reasons, reasons: stare
wrinkles
on cellophane, and
we are
     pinned
between sheets of glass,
turned
like dead slides, or
polarized
over fires
     fueled
by some crazy sawdust
stuffed
up all our dreams. . . .

Why should we
who
        dance
dying
through the air
pretend that questions mean
anything
more than whales
or flowers?
                Remember:
you flowed under my hand
in waterfalls, and
each pebble
of your breath
was a shape of laughter
younger
than despair.

Cappelbaum's Razor-Dance

This is my slashed
            face: pieces
of him over there,
the old man
with a green stone
in his eyes, when he complains
of girls
        cold
as crooked mountains, or

the soldier buttoned
with blood, metal studs
driven
into his brain:
maybe a physician
walking like a swollen kidney
into a world of General
Motors
        & love. . . .

and the woman
locked
behind the glass doors
of a library,
her breasts folded
like reference
books, a dream
smeared
on metal stacks. . . .

This is my slashed
face:
        the gown
of a bathed bride
falling out of the sky
with a smell
of rain, or
spiders
hanging from their own saliva
in the corners
of my father's lungs. . . .

and you,
              you : boasting
of true horizons,
a canopy
tighter
than your skin :
why are those bits of burning hair
blowing
from your mouth?

The Promontory

Silent

as the interior pain
under your skin,
behind your face : a wave
green
        white

starting
from nowhere, surf
on a pier, foam
bearing

drifted weeds
to your brain.

If a Cretan harp
unglued
under the blue spray
of your breath,

would each
             string

break

with a sound
of worms, squid
baited
        crucified
painted
with salt?

We angle
in the deep sea
of our flesh,
teeth,
        tubes:

a jellyfish

sucking
its thousand flowers
over our tongues.

Christmas Light Show

Projected on the damp crevices
of your thighs:
a random coagulation,
and the man with plates
slaps paint
on the plaster cave
of an empty hat factory: like

a priest
wiping himself
with the peeled skin
of an amoeba. . . .
        SQUISH
and the hot mouth
spits rainbows, breaking
into the drip
of a stretched kiss,
because
when you touch me, freaking
into space, your
lens
spreads over my face
and everybody skins
SANTA CLAUS
making it home. . . .

only one blackandwhite
Jew
        sits
with his head nailed
to his knees,
echoing
a bleached scream
at the moon.

Tasting Jenifer

Light-bags of space:
the sun
          rolling
between my toes. . . .
Olé! Olé!
and I ride her flesh
like a green bull
in a sea of
stars.

It's amazing, how
the mind
          quick
puffs in, flaring
a burst skin,
silver
spilled on a table,
all surfaces
folding

into tickled
silence:
          sometimes
I feel myself
like
strawberries.

Two for Freddie

I
When his mouth opens
around hello, he
circles the edge of his bones,
and I see them
hanging in a closet
whose door is never open,
a damp place
stuffed with old clothes
and bits of skin,
calculations
and mouldy rainbows
stretching
cramped muscles
across his face . . .

his smile
erupts on the membrane
of some gland I
don't
like to think about.

II
Olé, you constipated Jesuit!
where do all these
mem o randa
come from? do you
dream about them at night,
or write them
in your head
behind your eyeglasses
after you make
love?

Do you wear your eyeglasses
when you make love?
or your socks?
I ask this only to
reassure myself:
because there must be other
symptoms   nothing
after all
exists in a vacuum, not
even
         you.

Cappelbaum Drops Out

Never: because
the horizon is filled with exploding trees,
apples
mined with worms; because
when I run down the street
sniffing
fire hydrants,
a thousand dogs follow me
            screaming
about Love.

Sometimes
it's a fat policeman
who puffs up
Shirley Temple's brassiere, and issues
benedictions
from the tip of his club;

with mortgaged teeth he
threatens
to foreclose
on ABBERATIONS, like

that woman poet
with dead babies hanging from her mouth,
ripping
another foetus
from the torn placenta of Art;
she suffers, she
                    suffers
all over Asia,
while her conscience
flows
toward New England acreage. . . .
the singing Mother-Of-Us-All, her
in
dignation
knows no menopause.

Even the Flower People carry
knives
in their petals,
                    hustling
another chemical
or smearing themselves
over toilets without water, typewriters
without keys;
and in front of the Pentagon
bibles
spread themselves over the grass
like flaps of melted bones.

Meanwhile
the Black Brothers
dream of corpses, and play
with an Africa
whose taste would make them vomit; climbing
the unwashed names
of Arab slavers who cooked a continent,
they boil a crazy goulash
of non-history, and
march
        burning
up their own assholes.

Never, never: I will stand
nowhere
you can follow, you
whose brains
have turned into iron pipes, whose
hips   thighs   beards   dreams   legs
are printed
        like slogans
over all the sunlight and
possible
blue water of the world.

Cappelbaum's Resolution

An end to funny zoos:
no more queer animals
leaping like yellow

fleas
from the happy skin,
the balloon
of my tongue:
all the giraffes
with flowers growing on their hooves
have been drowned
in washing machines,
boiled
into soap.

I don't know: maybe
you are right, maybe
I have to bleed
bombjuice
all over my shirt. . . .
but why
do I feel like a torn placenta
flushed down the secret
plumbing
of God?

Once
I rode through the world
on my own back,
driving camels
through every part of the sea,
mounting whales
in subway stations, looking
behind the dry landscape
of your eye
for dolphins: for white birds
drunk
on seaweed and love.

Cappelbaum's Confession

I am wrong,
I am wrong,
I am wrong, I
admit it,
I am wrong:

I will go
and stand
under a black tree,
and let aphids
spray
nicotine over me. . . .

I will put coffee-
grinds
in my underwear,
and write shopping lists
on a typewriter
that doesn't have
keys. . . .

The ants
running over my desk
tell me I am
wrong,
the breakfast corpses
in my newspaper
tell me,
and the unpaid bills

stuffed
in the soap-box
of your face : all tell me
how
        goddamnit
and why
I am wrong, I am wrong, I am
wrong.

Cappelbaum at the Clavichord

I have dug a cave deep, deep in the convolutions
of my ear, away from voices
that hang from new jungles : this
my city
and the iron feathers of paradise,
flesh-eating birds
laying eggs in the mouth of History or God :
as though the air were filled with a winged octopus
cramming his legs
up all the crevices and joints of my life,
breaking open my pores : and from each of his mouths
a microphone appears, telling me
in what direction it is right and proper
to bleed.

I have made myself into a spiral staircase
carved from light,
and when I dance from one end to the other,
my life beating into space

like the sea caught in the shell of a dead man,
a breath greener than reason
clings to my face:
and the soldier, the Savior,
the woman
screaming from a balcony
(each hair of her love driven into an enemy's groin)
fall upon the roof of my canopy, my wedding flesh,
like headlines
broken by the wind.

Cappelbaum's Halloween

Take a trip
through a crazy zoo, where Tarzan
swings
from a rope of mafia-spaghetti,
where hyenas
                giggle
green feathers, and whales
pick their teeth
with a rainbow
of splintered trees, stones
peeled
like bananas. . . .

Chagall's rooster
stomps
over mountains
in white spats, a penguin

wearing Dali's mustache,
and in a thicket
of bamboo or rhododendrons,
tigers
lay speckled eggs
in a nest of Marshall McLuhan's hair:
each follicle electric
as Carnaby Street.

It's a roller-coaster
without tracks,
and the Man in the Painted Vest
runs backward, each leg
stuck
up a megaphone: he catches
flower-people, soldiers, Paul Goodman,
thieves, Nixon, polar-bears,
Mohammed Ali
(with a green fez over his fists)
as they drop from television towers,
complaining
of crab-lice on their testimonials.

Even Mao's proletarian underwear
appears
          like revelation
on Madison Avenue, in white silk,
and the discothique throwers
juggle chocolate-covered
corpses
on the bicycle paths of Central Park. . . .

Believe me, you don't need
cinemascope or funny
grass:

grab a clothesline, a copy
of the *New York Times,*
and pin yourself to a window-sill:
you'll dance,
                you'll dance
from your favorite peanut wagon,
with balloons
    popping
under the Happy Childhood
of your days and nights.

Cappelbaum's Harmonica

        HA! I could dimple
the world
if i wanted
                holes
where mountains are, and
    oceans
pouring
through the poles
like wine. . . .

it's decisions like
that
keep a man
swinging
over the green leaves
of his one-tree
forest.